HILARIOUS HOLIDAY HUMOR

JOKES FOR Halloween

Gareth Stevens PUBLISHING

BY JANE R. DAVIS

Please visit our website, www.garethstevens.com. For a free color catalog of all our high-quality books, call toll free 1-800-542-2595 or fax 1-877-542-2596.

Library of Congress Cataloging-in-Publication Data
Names: Davis, Jane R., author.
Title: Jokes for Halloween / Jane R. Davis.
Description: Buffalo, New York : Gareth Stevens Publishing, 2026. | Series: Hilarious holiday humor | Includes index. | Audience: Grades 2-3
Identifiers: LCCN 2024050734 (print) | LCCN 2024050735 (ebook) | ISBN 9781482471939 (library binding) | ISBN 9781482471922 (paperback) | ISBN 9781482471946 (ebook)
Subjects: LCSH: Halloween–Juvenile humor. | LCGFT: Humor.
Classification: LCC PN6231.H316 R35 2026 (print) | LCC PN6231.H316 (ebook) | DDC 818/.602–dc23/eng/20241028
LC record available at https://lccn.loc.gov/2024050734
LC ebook record available at https://lccn.loc.gov/2024050735

Published in 2026 by
Gareth Stevens Publishing
2544 Clinton Street
Buffalo, NY 14224

Designer: Leslie Taylor
Editor: Kristen Rajczak Nelson

Photo credits: Cover (cartoon objects) Natalllenka.m/Shutterstock.com, (vintage ghost) Vector Tradition/Shutterstock.com; series art (font) TortugaStudios/Shutterstock.com, (laughing emojis) Setia Abadi Art/Shutterstock.com, (shapes) Kseniia Belka/Shutterstock.com; p. 5 FamVeld/Shutterstock.com; p. 6 Brilliant Eye/Shutterstock.com; p. 7 Richafuji/Shutterstock.com; p. 8 Shutterstock AI Generator/Shutterstock.com; p. 9 (dracula costume) Ollyy/Shutterstock.com, (inset poster) Universal Pictures/File:Dracula (1931 film poster - Style F).jpg_commons.wikimedia.org, (inset film) Unknown Author/File:Lupita Tovar and Carlos Villarías in Dracula (1931 spanish film).jpg_commons.wikimedia.org; p. 10 Joseph Sorrentino/Shutterstock.com; p. 11 (halloween decor) Aaron of L.A. Photography/Shutterstock.com, (funny skeleton) Volodymyr TVERDOKHLIB/Shutterstock.com; p. 12 Mashaki/Shutterstock.com; p. 13 (witch) Ironika/Shutterstock.com (Wizard of Oz) Insomnia Cured Here/Flickr.com; p. 14 (toy) Forest_Fairy/Shutterstock.com, (clay zombie) stasB/Shutterstock.com; p. 15 (bottom) Universal Studios/File:Son-of-frankenstein.jpg_commons.wikimedia.org, (inset top) Universal Pictures/File:Son-of-frankenstein.jpg_commons.wikimedia.org, (inset Frankenstein head) Universal Studios, NBCUniversal/File:Frankenstein's monster (Boris Karloff).jpg_wikimedia.org; p. 16 (lake) FOTOKITA/Shutterstock.com, (werewolf) Jean-Claude Caprara/Shutterstock.com; p. 17 Rabid Fables Collective/Shutterstock.com; p. 18 KM-Photography/Shutterstock.com; p. 19 Teri Virbickis/Shutterstock.com; p. 20 AYO Production/Shutterstock.com; p. 29 Evgeny Atamanenko/Shutterstock.com.

Printed in the United States of America

CPSIA compliance information: Batch #CSGS26: For further information contact Gareth Stevens at 1-800-542-2595.

CONTENTS

BOLDFACE WORDS APPEAR IN THE GLOSSARY.

Halloween Fun!

From haunted hayrides to homemade costumes, there are many ways to enjoy Halloween! It's a holiday **celebrated** on October 31. Kids across the United States dress up and go trick-or-treating to gather as much candy as they can carry!

The beginnings of this spooky holiday date back hundreds of years. In the past, the last day of October was called All Hallows Eve, or the day people believed spirits wandered the Earth. Today, the ghosts that wander about are probably kids in costume!

Ghosts, witches, and other spooky creatures are popular Halloween costumes. But you can dress as anything you want!

LET'S CELEBRATE!

Some Halloween ideas come from the holiday Samhain celebrated by the **Celtic** people. It started their new year.

GHOSTLY GIGGLES

Why didn't the ghost have fun at the party?

He had no body to dance with.

Why did the ghost blow his nose?

It was full of boo-gers.

Where do ghosts shop?

They visit the ghost-ery store.

What game should you play with a baby ghost?

Peek-a-boo.

Do you believe in ghosts? A poll done in 2019 said about 46 percent of Americans do!

LET'S CELEBRATE!

El Día de los Muertos, or the Day of the Dead, is celebrated from midnight on October 31 to November 2. Mexican families make offerings to the spirits of those who have died and can visit Earth for this time each year.

SILLY OR SCARY?

How do vampires travel?

They take blood vessels.

Why didn't you invite Dracula to our party?

He's a pain in the neck.

What fruit do vampires like?

They enjoy neck-tarines.

What does a vampire use to lock his door?

A dead bolt.

The famous movie *Dracula* came out in 1931. It was based on a book that came out in 1897. There have been many **versions** of the Dracula character since!

LET'S CELEBRATE!

A vampire is a **fantasy** creature that drinks the blood of living animals and humans. It is known for its fangs, or long sharp teeth.

TICKLE THE FUNNY BONE

Skeletons are common Halloween **decorations**. They can be super spooky or super silly!

GET WITCHY!

Have you ever seen twin witches?

You can't tell which witch is which!

What's wrong with a flat witch's hat?

It has no point.

What subject at school do witches like best?

Spelling.

Does a witch keep her vehicle in a garage?

No, the broom closet.

Today, witches are often shown with green skin and pointy hats and noses. This may go back to the way the Wicked Witch of the West was shown in the 1939 movie *The Wizard of Oz*.

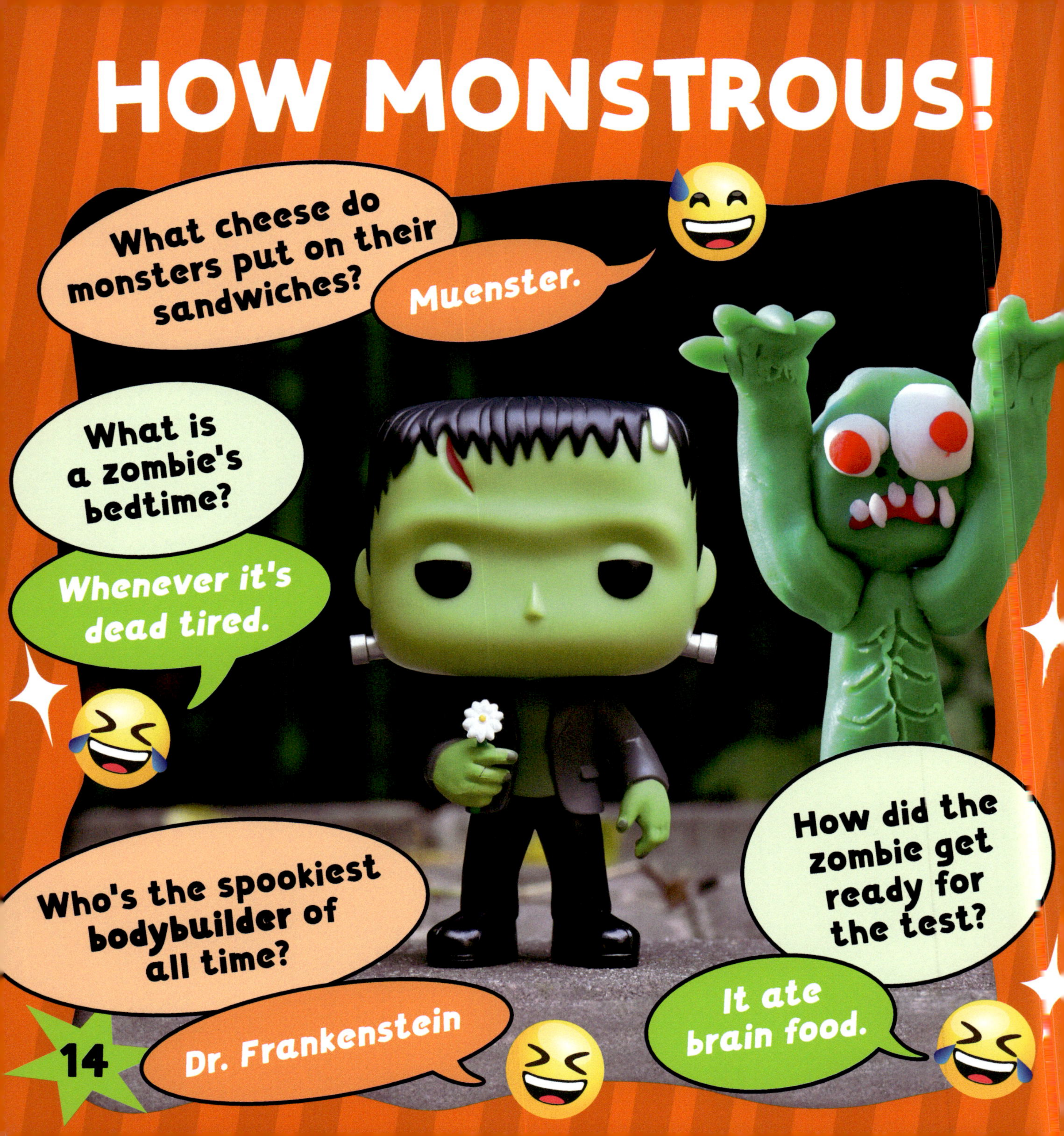

HOW MONSTROUS!

What cheese do monsters put on their sandwiches?

Muenster.

What is a zombie's bedtime?

Whenever it's dead tired.

Who's the spookiest bodybuilder of all time?

Dr. Frankenstein

How did the zombie get ready for the test?

It ate brain food.

There have been many movies made about Frankenstein and his monster, including this one from the 1930s!

LET'S CELEBRATE!

When we say "Frankenstein" today, it may mean a big, scary monster. But in the book *Frankenstein*, which first came out in 1818, Victor Frankenstein is actually the man who made the monster!

DOGGONE FUNNY

Why are werewolves always late?

Because they're not when wolves.

How did the werewolf party go?

It was a howling success.

What's the best Halloween vacation spot?

Lake Eerie.

The full moon comes around about once a month. If werewolves were real, we'd hear about them more than just at Halloween!

PUMPKIN TIME

What did the pumpkin say to the person carving it?

Cut that out!

Why did the jack-o-lantern get scared?

It had no guts.

How do you fix a jack-o-lantern?

You use a pumpkin patch.

Knock, Knock!

Who's There?

Pumpkin.

Pumpkin who?

Knock, Knock!

Who's There?

Pumpkin.

Pumpkin who?

Jack-o'-lanterns like these have been **carved** in the United States since the mid-1800s.

Knock, Knock!

Who's There?

Orange.

Orange who?

Orange you glad I didn't say pumpkin?

FAIRLY SCARY

Why did they need a fence around the graveyard?

Because people were dying to get in.

Who did the little monster cry for late at night?

His mummy.

Knock, Knock!

Who's There?

Phillip!

Phillip who?

Phillip my bag with candy!

LET'S CELEBRATE!

Trick-or-treating became popular in the United States around the 1950s.

Halloween can be spooky and creepy or just for fun! How will you celebrate?

GLOSSARY

bodybuilder: One who builds a body. Also, a person who exercises and eats in certain ways to grow their muscles.

carve: To cut into.

celebrate: To honor with special activities.

Celtic: Having to do with the Celts, a group of people who lived from Europe to Asia in ancient times.

decoration: Something that makes a home or place look better.

fantasy: Having to do with things that are imaginary.

howling: Great. Also, making a sound like a howl, or doglike sound.

vehicle: An object that moves people from one place to another.

version: A form of something that is different from others.

vessel: A tube that carries blood throughout the body. Also, a boat.

FOR MORE INFORMATION

Books

Owell, Elle. *Spooky Jokes for Kids*. London, UK: Orchard Books, 2024.

Roza, Greg. *20 Fun Facts About Halloween*. Buffalo, NY: Gareth Stevens Publishing, 2025.

Websites

A History of the Halloween Costume
https://childrenstheatre.org/2023/10/26/a-history-of-the-halloween-costume/
Check out the beginnings of Halloween costumes in this article.

The History of Halloween
https://kpcnotebook.scholastic.com/post/history-halloween
Read more about Halloween here.

Publisher's note to educators and parents: Our editors have carefully reviewed these websites to ensure that they are suitable for students. Many websites change frequently, however, and we cannot guarantee that a site's future contents will continue to meet our high standards of quality and educational value. Be advised that students should be closely supervised whenever they access the internet.

INDEX